THE WORLD OF WORK

MINE

PHILIP SAUVAIN

Editorial planning
Philip Steele

SILVER BURDETT PRESS

Copyright © 1988 by Schoolhouse Press, Inc.
an imprint of Silver Burdett Inc.
Prentice Hall Building, Route 9W,
Englewood Cliffs, N.J. 07632

Original copyright, © Macmillan Education Limited 1988
© BLA Publishing Limited 1988

All rights reserved. No reproduction, copy or transmission of this publication may be made without written permission.

No paragraph of this publication may be reproduced, copied or transmitted save with written permission of the publisher.

Designed and produced by BLA Publishing Limited, East Grinstead, Sussex, England.

A Ling Kee Company

Illustrations by Steve Lings/Linden Artists; Sebastian Quigley/Linden Artists and Sallie Alane Reason
Printed in Hong Kong

88/89/90/91/92/93   6 5 4 3 2 1

Library of Congress Cataloging-in-Publication Data

Sauvain, Philip Arthur
    In a mine.
    (The World of work)
    Includes index.
    Summary: Surveys the history of coal mining and describes how it works, how a mine is designed and constructed, and how the coal is sorted, treated, and moved.
    1. Mining engineering — Juvenile literature.
[1. Coal mines and mining. 2. Mining engineering]
I. Title. II. Series.
TN148.S28   1988   622'.334   88-4534
ISBN 0-382-09723-8

Photographic credits

t = top *b* = bottom *l* = left *r* = right

cover: National Coal Board

4*t* British Coal; 4*b*, 5 ZEFA; 6, 7 Vivien Fifield; 9 ZEFA; 10*t*, 10*b*, 11 British Coal; 14*t* Barnaby's Picture Library; 14*b* British Coal; 15 Conoco Inc; 16, 17, 18 British Coal; 19 Conoco Inc; 20 British Coal; 21 ZEFA; 22, 23 Conoco Inc; 24 Vision International; 25*t* Conoco Inc; 25*b* British Coal; 26*t* ZEFA; 26*b* Conoco Inc; 27 ZEFA; 28*t* British Coal; 28*b* ZEFA; 29 Rex Features; 31*t*, 31*b* British Coal; 32, 33*t* ZEFA; 33*l* British Coal; 33*r* ZEFA; 34, 35*t*, 35*b*, 36, 37, 38*t* British Coal; 38*b* ZEFA; 39 Conoco Inc; 40 British Coal; 41*t*, 41*b* Conoco Inc; 42 Trevor Hill; 43*t* Science Photo Library; 43*b* Rex Features; 44 Turners Ltd

How To Use This Book:
This book has many useful features. For example, look at the table of contents. See how it describes each section in the book. Find a section you want to read and turn to it.
    Notice that the section is a "two-page spread." That is, it covers two facing pages. Now look at the headings in the spread. Headings are useful when you want to locate specific information. Next, look at a photograph, drawing, chart or map and find its caption. Captions give you additional information. A chart or map may also have labels to help you.
    Scan the spread for a word in **bold print**. If you cannot find one in this spread, find one in another spread. Bold-print words are defined in the glossary at the end of the book. Find your bold-print word in the glossary.
    Now turn to the index at the end of the book. When you have a specific topic or subject to research, look for it in the index. you will quickly know whether the topic is in the book.
    We hope you will use the features in this book to help you learn about new and exciting things.

Contents

Introduction	4	Coming off Shift	28
Miners in the Past	6	Coal near the Surface	30
Around the World	8	Coal at the Surface	32
Searching for Coal	10	Emergency!	34
How a Coal Mine Works	12	Separating and Cleaning Coal	36
Down the Shaft	14	Moving Coal	38
Avoiding Danger Below	16	Restoring the Land	40
Health and Safety	18	The Hidden Cost of Coal	42
A Wall of Coal	20	The Future	44
Chambers of Coal	22		
A New Coal Face	24	Glossary	46
Underground Travel	26	Index	48

Introduction

Thousands of people work in mines around the world. They dig out the rocklike material called **coal** which is used to provide heat and light and to make machines work. These people are called miners, and they play a very important part in the world of work today.

How Coal Was Made

Coal was formed millions of years ago. At that time, trees and plants grew in the hot, wet forests that covered most of the earth. When the trees died, they fell into muddy swamps and sank. Slowly, over millions of years, the trees were buried under mud and rocks. As the rocks pressed down on the trees, the trees changed into the hard brown or black material called coal. Coal is a **fossil fuel**.

▲ As one shift of miners finishes work, another shift prepares to take its place underground. Coal is one of the most useful fuels we have.

▼ Today, women work in many of the world's coal mines. This woman miner is working at a mine in Kentucky.

Introduction

How Coal Is Used

Most of the coal which is dug out of the ground is used to make electricity. The coal is taken to **power plants** where it is burned. Then, the electricity is used to light and heat homes, schools, hospitals, and factories. Electricity is also used to make trains run.

Coal is used to make steel, along with all kinds of other things, such as paints, glue, and make-up. It is even used to make clothes and soap!

A Working Life

Miners cut the coal underground and send it up to the surface. It sounds like a simple job. In fact, it takes a lot of skill and a lot of hard work. You can get an idea of what the job of coal miners is like if you look at their working clothes. Their helmets protect them against injury from falling rocks and their goggles keep flying dust out of their eyes. Their kneepads keep their knees from being scraped and cut if the miners have to crawl along a narrow tunnel. They also wear strong boots with steel toe caps to protect their feet. Mining is a dangerous job.

All Kinds of Jobs

The work in a mine never stops. Each miner works for several hours at a time. This period of time is called a **shift**. Some miners cut coal out of the ground at the **coal face**. These miners are called **faceworkers**. Some workers drive the trains and trucks which carry the coal around underground. Other workers make sure that the machinery is working safely and repair it when it breaks down.

Above the ground, mine workers also have important jobs to do. Some people work the machines which take miners to and from the coal face, or bring the coal to the surface. Others clean and separate the different types of coal before it is sold. Some people use computers to plan the work of the mine. Other people have jobs like typing letters, making meals, and cleaning the buildings. A team of people makes sure that safety rules are being followed. Another team takes care of the health of the workers. The men and women who do all these jobs are carefully trained for their work. Some of them will spend weeks, months, or even years learning more about their jobs in the mine.

▶ Miners repair machinery at a coal mine in New Zealand. Mining can be tiring, dirty, and sometimes dangerous work.

Miners in the Past

The first people to find coal may have been searching for wood to burn on a fire. They may have picked up pieces of coal on the seashore, or in places where a rockfall had broken off bits of coal.

Somehow, they found out that pieces of this hard, black, shiny rock would burn. Coal gave off more heat than wood, and it kept the fire going for a longer time. People wanted to use more of this coal, so they began to look for it. They found the coal in layers, called **seams**, between other rocks. When they dug out the coal, they became the first miners.

Old mine workings have been found which show that coal was being used a long time ago. The Romans mined coal about 1,600 years ago. The North American Hopi Indians and the Chinese mined coal, too.

The First Pits

When there was no more coal on the surface, miners dug down to reach the coal under the ground. First, they dug a hole, or **shaft**, about three to six yards deep. Then, they used rope ladders to go up and down the shaft. The miners who worked at the bottom of the shaft used pointed tools, or **picks**, to dig out the coal. As they dug, they hollowed out a bell-shaped pit. Because of this shape, these early mines were called **bell pits**.

When the miners had taken out as much coal as they could without causing the roof to fall in, they left the mine and dug a new bell pit. They filled the old pit up with earth from the new pit.

▼ This is a coal mine about 150 years ago. Smoke is coming from the boiler house. That is where the steam which worked the pumps was made.

Miners in the Past

Water in the Workings

The miners who dug these early pits found that water often filled up their mines. Sometimes, the pit flooded quickly and miners were drowned. They had to find a way to get rid of the water and keep the pit dry. The first machine to do this was a steam **pump** which was invented by an engineer named Thomas Newcomen nearly 300 years ago. He burned coal to heat water. The hot water made steam which drove the pump.

Coal for Machines

From the early 1700s, with the use of pumps, miners could dig deeper pits without the fear of flooding. They were able to mine coal, which was burned to make steam power to work new machines. The machines were used in factories as well as in mines.

In the mid-1800s, coal was also used as the fuel for steam trains and steamships. More and more coal was needed, so more pits were opened.

A Life of Hardship

There was a great deal of money to be made from selling coal. The owners of the new pits hired men, women, and even children to work in them. The miners had to work for up to twelve hours at a time. Children and women dragged hand trucks along tracks to the bottom of the shaft. There were often accidents. Hand trucks knocked people down or ran over fingers or toes. There were roof cave-ins and floods.

These new mines brought new dangers. They were much deeper than the old bell pits. Miners had to have more light to work with, so they used candles. Gases trapped in the coal seams exploded when candle flames or sparks set them on fire. Other gases choked the miners when they breathed them in. In 1815, Humphrey Davy invented the **safety lamp**. The flame changed color if there was any poisonous gas in the mines.

Today, coal mines are much safer to work in, but there are still many accidents every year.

▶ The first mine railroads used ponies to pull the trucks of coal. The workings were lit by candles. Sometimes, underground gas caught fire. Explosions were common and many miners were killed.

Around the World

Coal miners work in most countries of the world. Some miners cut coal in Australia, China, and the USSR. Others work in coal mines in India, Africa, Europe, North America, and South America. Some even work in the ice and snow near the Arctic Circle.

There are many different ways of cutting coal. The method used depends on how deep and thick the coal is below the ground and on the type of coal.

▼ The earth was much warmer millions of years ago. Tropical forests grew in many parts of the world. The forests have now gone, but their trees have turned into coal. That is why coalfields can be found in every continent today.

Types of Coal

Some miners work in mines which produce soft brown coal. This is called **lignite**. Brown coal is easy to mine because it is close to the surface. However, it does not give off as much heat as black coal.

Some miners work with a very hard coal called **anthracite**. This coal gives off more heat than any other coal, but it is difficult to mine. The seams are often far below the earth's surface. Sometimes, the seams are not level like those in other coal mines.

Most miners dig **bituminous coal**. This is the coal used in power plants and for making steel.

Where Coal Is Found

Three countries, China, the United States and the USSR, own ninety percent of the world's coal.

In the United States, coalfields stretch from Pennsylvania in the east to the prairies in the west and as far north as Alaska.

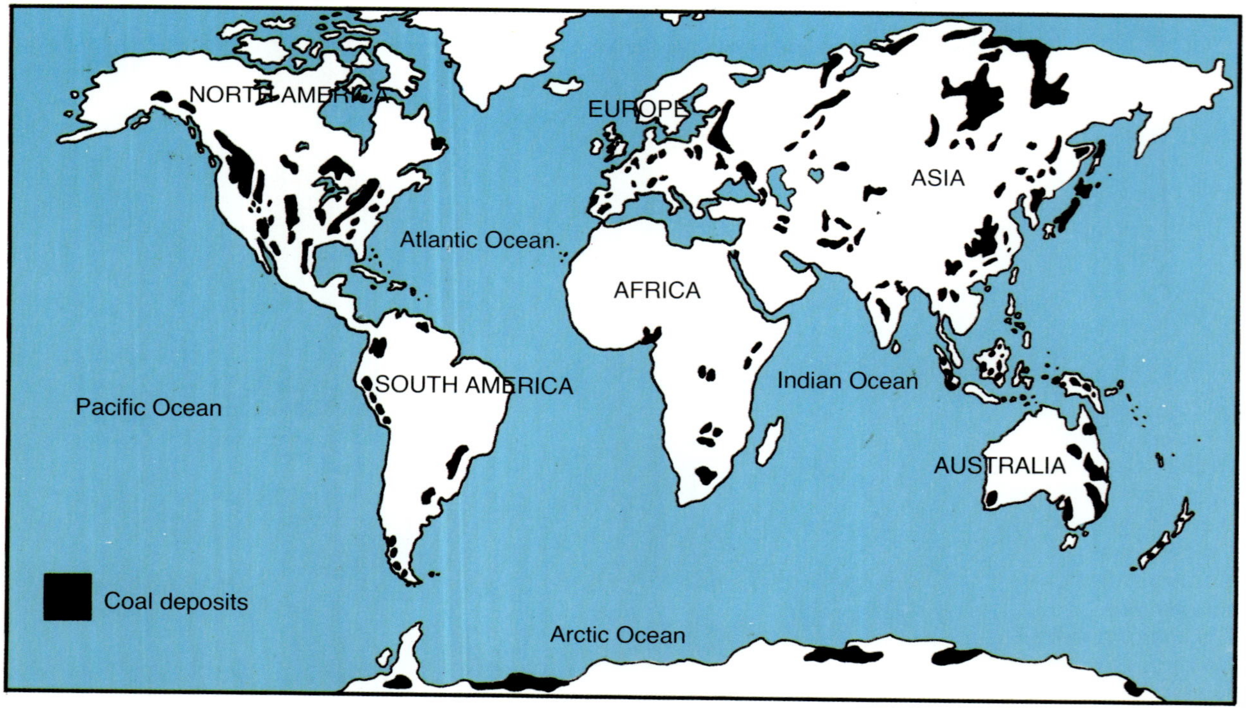

Around the World

The North American coalfields, as well as those in Australia and India, have thick seams of coal which are not far below the surface. Coalfields in other parts of the world, such as Europe and the USSR, have thin seams of coal deep underground.

There may be 10 million tons of coal left in the world. This amount of coal could last about 250 years. Luckily, much of the world's coal is found in thick layers on or near the surface.

▶ These miners are working in a coal mine in South Africa. South Africa contains about 97 percent of Africa's known coal reserves.

▼ This diagram shows you which countries produce the most coal. Each lump of coal is equal to about 120 million tons of coal.

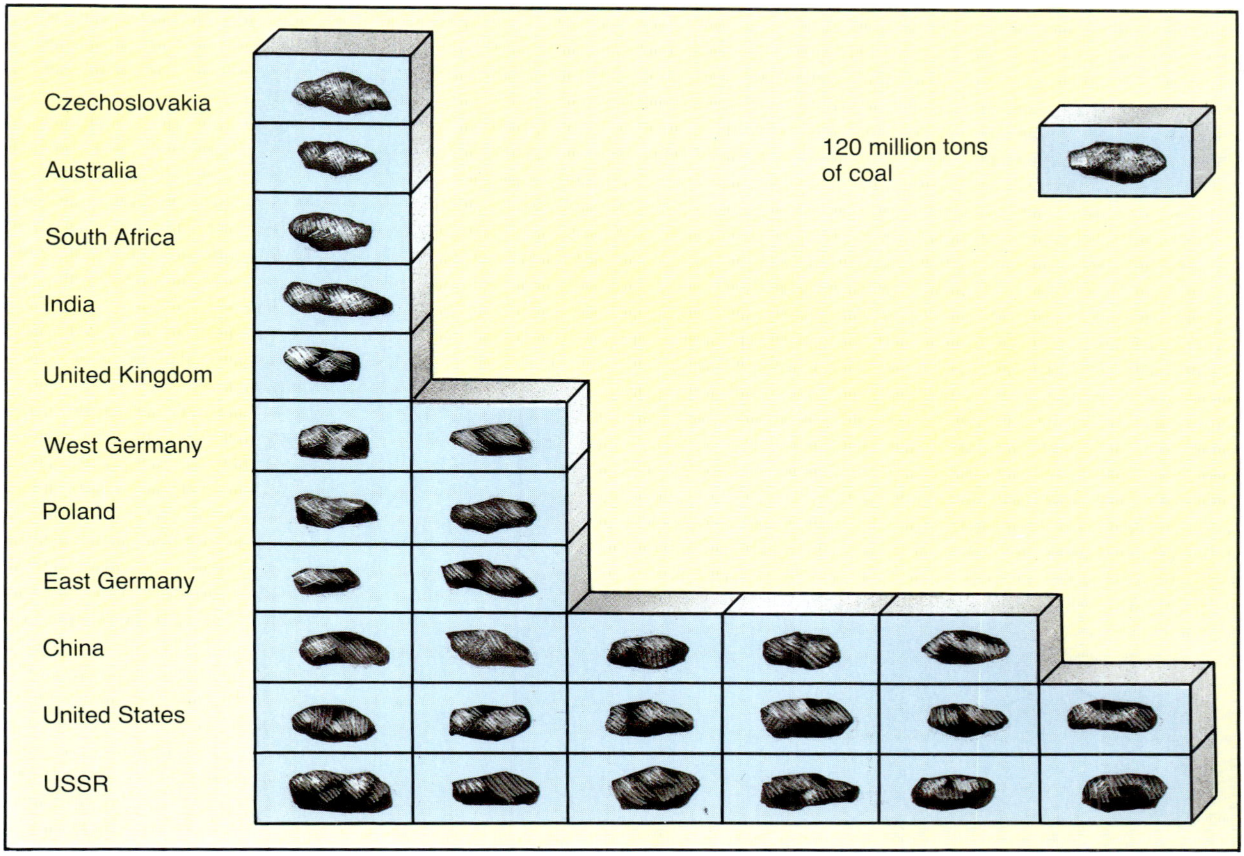

Searching for Coal

Most people would not know if there was a coal seam in the earth beneath them. This is why the companies who run the coal mines employ scientists. These scientists are called **geologists**. The geologists study the earth and figure out where coal is likely to be found. They can also find out how deep the coal seams are below the ground.

The geologists figure out if the seams of coal are straight and flat. Sometimes, movements of the earth make the seam uneven, or **folded**. Folded seams are hard to mine since they slope up and then slope down.

▲ A geologist prepares a seismic survey. The result of the survey will be analysed by a computer. It will provide diagrams showing the layout and depths of underground coal and the position of any major faults.

◀ Samples of rock are pushed up through hollow pipes as the drill bites into the earth. Geologists test the samples to see whether there is coal in the rocks.

Searching for Coal

► Geologists study the results of a seismic survey. The patterns on the paper show that there might be coal in the earth below.

Testing for Coal

Geologists start their search by looking at special maps. The maps show all the different kinds of rock which make up the earth. They also show places where coal has been mined already.

The geologists drill rows of small holes in the ground where they think there may be coal. Then, they set off explosions inside these holes. They measure the way the noise travels through the rocks under the ground. This is called a **seismic survey**. It helps the geologists to figure out whether they are likely to find coal seams under the ground.

Drilling for Coal

The only certain way to find out if there is coal in the ground is to take samples of the rocks. Mining engineers set up a **drilling rig** to do this. They use a drill which has diamonds on the end of it. Diamonds are used because they are very hard and will cut through rocks easily. The drill cuts a thin hole deep into the rocks below the earth's surface. This hole is called a **borehole**. As the drill bores through the ground, the workers attach lengths of hollow pipe onto the drill to make it longer.

The drill cuts a long strip of rock out of the ground. This is called the **core sample**. If they find coal in the core sample, the geologists measure it to see how thick and how deep the coal seams are. They drill other boreholes to find out the size of the coalfield.

If the coalfield is small and very deep, it may cost too much money to build a mine to get the coal out. If it is a large coalfield, or the coal is near the surface, then a new mine will be opened.

Opening up a Mine

People who decide where the tunnels will be drilled underground are called **surveyors**. They keep the maps and plans of the mine up-to-date. When the earth moves, the tunnels may become unsafe. They must be closed and new tunnels opened up. Surveyors will draw up new plans for this work. It is also important for the mine workers' safety to be able to see all the tunnels on paper. If there is an accident, rescue workers have to know how to reach miners who may be trapped.

How a Coal Mine Works

The area with buildings on it at the top of a coal mine is the **pithead**.

The control room is at the mine pithead. The people who work there use computers to plan the work of the mine and to work some of the machinery. Television screens show the control room workers what is happening in other parts of the mine. All the machinery in the mine is run by electricity which can be switched on or off from the control room. Computers help to make the mine safe.

▼ A mine covers a huge area. Here, the shaft has been drawn much shorter than it really is, so that you can see the work of the miners underground as well as on the surface.

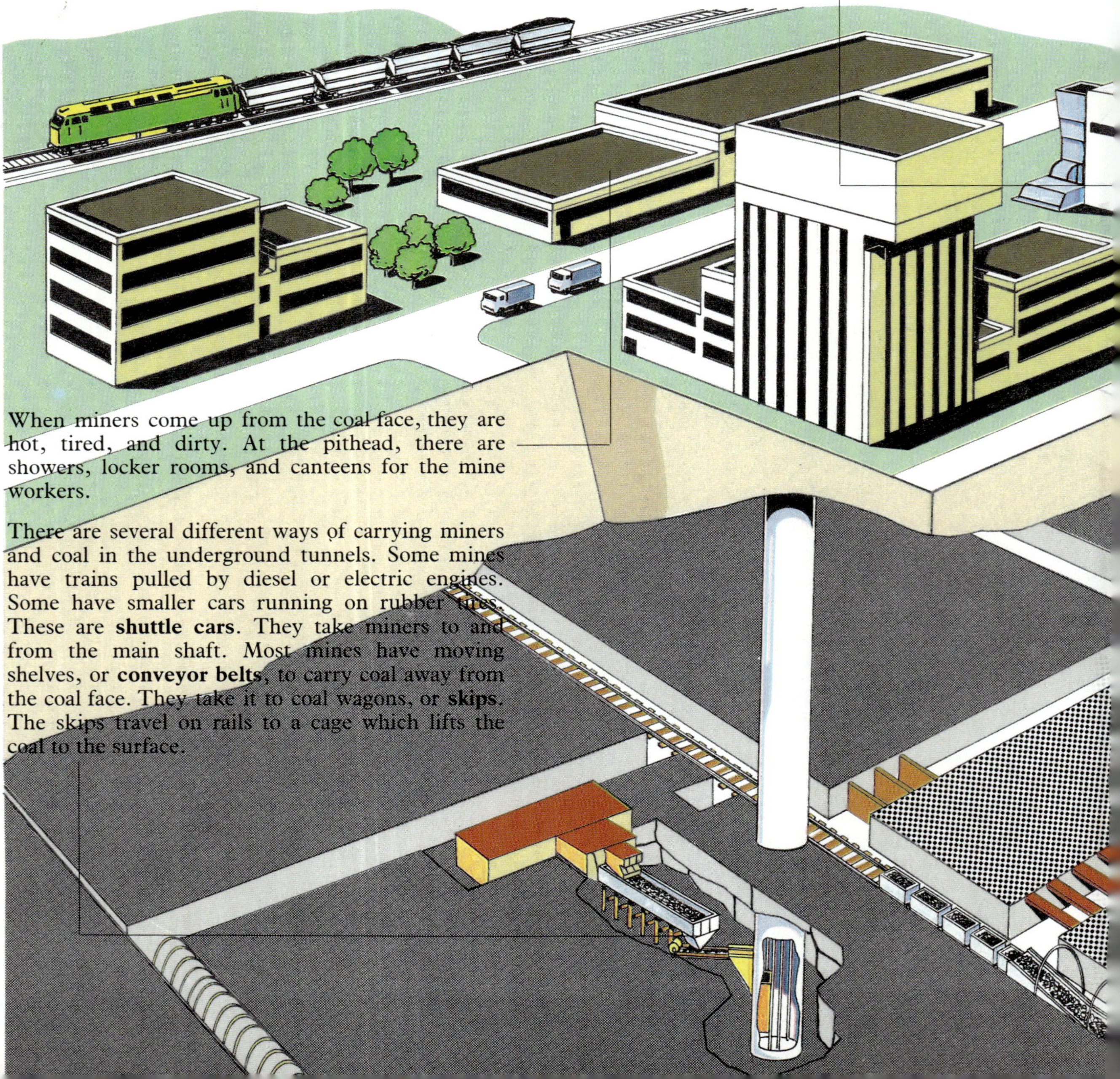

When miners come up from the coal face, they are hot, tired, and dirty. At the pithead, there are showers, locker rooms, and canteens for the mine workers.

There are several different ways of carrying miners and coal in the underground tunnels. Some mines have trains pulled by diesel or electric engines. Some have smaller cars running on rubber tires. These are **shuttle cars**. They take miners to and from the main shaft. Most mines have moving shelves, or **conveyor belts**, to carry coal away from the coal face. They take it to coal wagons, or **skips**. The skips travel on rails to a cage which lifts the coal to the surface.

How a Coal Mine Works

Miners travel to and from the mine workings in an elevator, or **cage**. The cage is raised and lowered up and down the mine's main shaft. This shaft also takes fresh air to the tunnels. Large fans at the pithead blow fresh air into the mine. Another shaft takes the used air up to the surface. This movement of fresh air through the mine is called **ventilation**.

At the pithead are the huge wheels which wind up the steel ropes, or **cables**, which lift the coal and the miners to the surface. This is the **winding gear**. A winding engineer's job is to take care of these wheels and to work the winding gear.

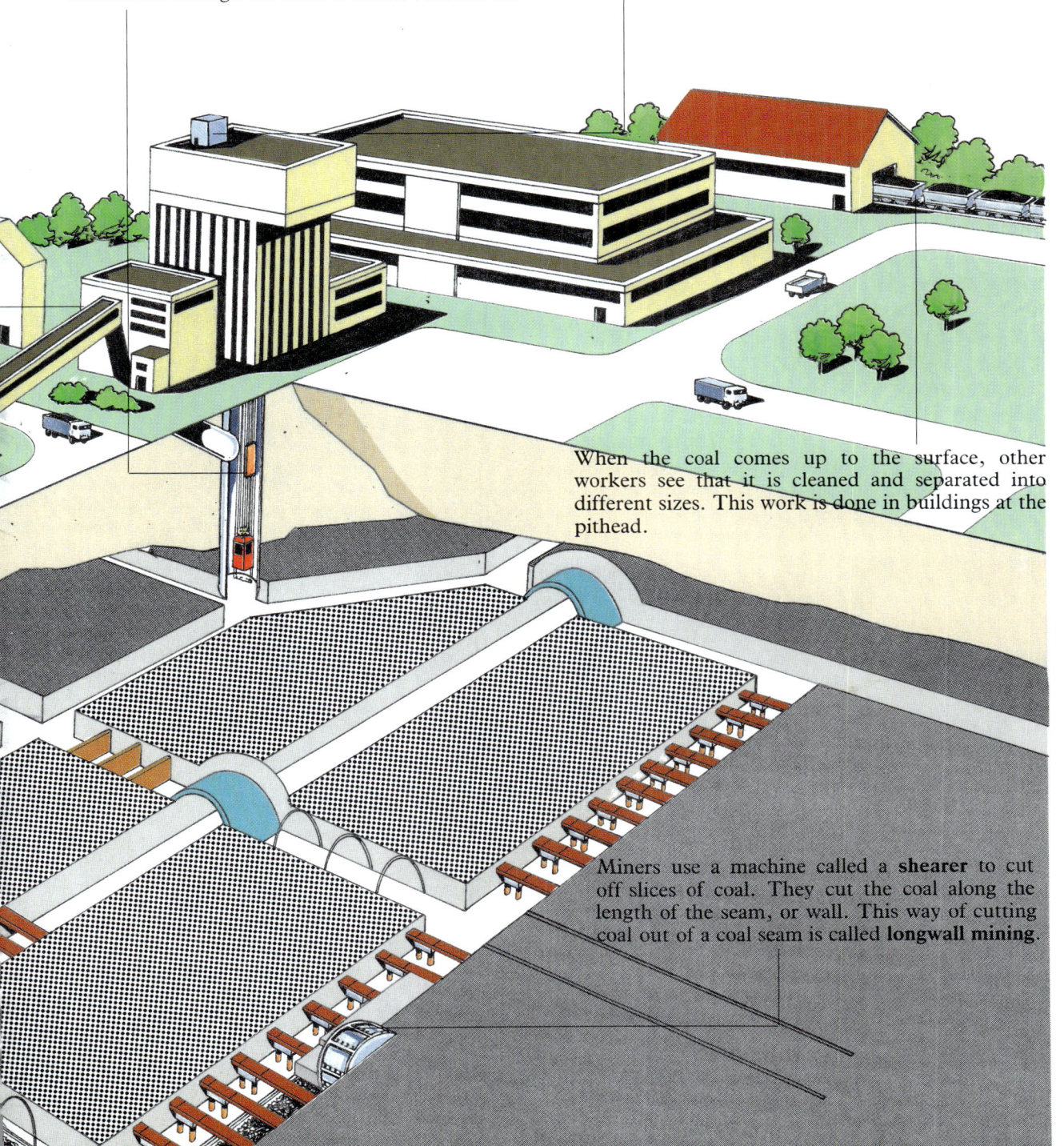

When the coal comes up to the surface, other workers see that it is cleaned and separated into different sizes. This work is done in buildings at the pithead.

Miners use a machine called a **shearer** to cut off slices of coal. They cut the coal along the length of the seam, or wall. This way of cutting coal out of a coal seam is called **longwall mining**.

Down the Shaft

Even though the work of a coal mine is done mainly under the ground, there are many buildings at the pithead. The tallest buildings are the ones which hold the winding gear.

Winding Gear

The winding gear is made up of wheels which wind up and let down long lengths of strong steel cable. These are called lifting ropes. It is the winding engineer's job to make sure that the cages and skips are raised and lowered safely at the right speed.

Some mines still have wheels on top of tall open frames. You can see the wheels spinning around when the winding gear is working. In coal mines today, the winding gear is usually built inside a tall tower called the **winding house**.

▲ The winding house rises high above the mine, marking the site of the main shaft. It houses the wheels which lower or raise the cage.

◀ The winding engineer controls the machinery which lowers the cage down the shaft. Here you can see the large wheels of the winding gear.

Down the Shaft

▲ Miners wait to enter the cage. Attached to their helmets are ear protectors which the miners put over their ears when they are working with noisy machinery.

Going Down

Two hundred years ago, miners were carried down the mine shaft in large buckets. Small children held on tightly to each other as they were lowered down on chains into the darkness below. They were lucky! Some miners had to climb down ladders. They carried the coal up to the surface in baskets on their backs.

Today, the cage at a coal mine carries about sixty miners and their equipment up and down the shaft in safety. The cage is usually about six yards wide. Many cages have two floors, so that two groups of miners can be carried at the same time.

Visitors who have never been down a coal mine usually find the journey in the cage very exciting. The doors clang shut and the cage drops swiftly down the shaft. People can see the shaft wall as they drop. Most mines in the United States are about 300 feet deep. In the United Kingdom, many mines are more than four times as deep as this.

Avoiding Danger Below

In the past, many accidents were caused by flooding and by explosions. Sometimes, miners were choked by gases or by the smoke from an underground fire. Rock falls sometimes sealed off a part of a mine and trapped the miners inside. A hundred years ago, mining disasters with a large loss of life were far too common.

The world's worst mining disaster took place nearly fifty years ago. Coal dust exploded at the Hinkeiko coal mine in China on April 26, 1942. Almost 1,600 miners were killed.

Fresh Air

Today, officials take great care to make sure that the mine workings are well ventilated. The miners sink two shafts when opening a new coal mine. Fresh air enters the mine down the downcast shaft. The old, stale, and used air is pushed up the upcast shaft to the surface where it escapes into the air outside. Good ventilation in a mine gets rid of the dangerous **methane gas**, which can cause explosions. Ventilation also keeps the coal mine free from the other gases which could suffocate the miners.

▼ This equipment is used to test the air in the mine for gas. It is linked to small computers which will set off alarms and switch off power if dangerous levels of gas are detected.

Avoiding Danger Below

▲ This machinery is used to pump water from the mine workings to the surface.

Pumping Water

Mine officials must also make sure that the mine has a good way of getting rid of any water which might flood the workings. Most mines today have drains which get rid of any water that may leak into the mine. The water collects in drains, or sumps, below the shafts. From the sumps, the water is pumped to the surface.

No Flames

In many mines, the miners are searched before they are allowed to go underground to make sure that they are not carrying cigarettes or matches. A flame could cause the methane gas in a coal mine to explode. Even a tiny spark could set off an explosion. Cables and electrical connections which might cause sparks are hidden behind special fireproof coverings. Conveyor belts run on rubber rollers and shuttle cars use rubber wheels. This lessens the risk that moving metal might make sparks, too.

Special instruments, called **sensors**, are also used underground. Some sensors detect smoke, or measure small rises in temperature which could mean that a fire has started. Some sensors can also detect levels of methane gas in the air. The sensors sound the alarm if there is smoke, too much heat, or too much methane. Their measurements also show up on the control room screens, so that safety officials can deal with any problem quickly.

# Health and Safety

The clothes and equipment the miners wear helps to protect them while they are underground. They wear thick gloves to keep their hands from getting cut. Their helmets, or hard hats, protect their heads from falling rocks. Each helmet has a light clipped to it which lights the way in dark tunnels. This means that wherever the miner looks, the lamp will always throw light where it is needed but their hands are left free to operate machinery.

Checking In

Mine officials need to know who is working down the mine on each shift in case there is an accident. In some countries, such as Britain, mines use a special way of keeping track of people. At the start of a shift, each miner is given two identical tally counters which are marked with the miner's number or name. Before entering the cage, the miner hands in one of the tally counters to a clerk. At the end of the shift, as they come out of the cage, the miners hand in the second counter. The clerk then matches up the pairs of counters. If there is only one counter for someone who should have come off from a shift, a search party is sent out.

◀ Miners must wear special clothing to protect them when they are working. Note the helmets with lamps, the knee pads, and the strong boots.

Health and Safety

▲ A miner collects his tally. The tally system helps mine officials know that each miner has returned safely from underground.

Miners' Health

The company doctor is in charge of the health of all the workers in the mine. In large mines, there is a medical center at the pithead where a team of workers is always ready to deal with any medical problems the miners may have.

The company doctor is trained especially to work in a mine. In some countries, the doctor goes to meetings with other mine officials, where the health and safety of the mine is discussed. All officials are trained in **first aid**, and the company doctor teaches new workers what to do if there is a bad accident.

In some countries, the company doctor will also go underground to check the first aid stations. Today, most underground accidents are not very bad. The bandages which miners need are kept at the first aid stations. There are pain-killing drugs there, in case there is a more serious injury. The company doctor teaches miners how to give injections of these drugs.

Miners go to the medical center with all kinds of problems. They may have sprained backs or pulled muscles from the heavy work they do. They may have coughs or colds or other illnesses. Sometimes, they just want advice about their health.

The Medical Team

The medical aides attend training courses to learn about new drugs and new safety methods. They must keep up-to-date.

If there is a bad accident, people will have to be taken to the hospital. Therefore, in some countries, some miners are also trained as ambulance drivers. They carry a box with them which is like a small radio. It is called a pager, and it bleeps when they are needed.

A Wall of Coal

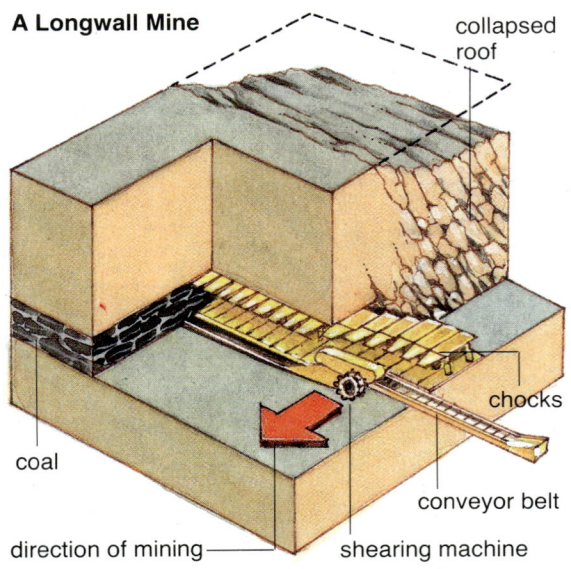

A Longwall Mine

Miners take a lot of care to make sure the roofs of their tunnels are as strong as possible. In some mines, they do this by not digging out some of the coal in a seam. They leave half the coal in place, so that it forms blocks or pillars to support the roof. This is the **room and pillar** method of mining.

The other way, used by most miners in Europe, the USSR, and more and more in North America, is the longwall method of mining.

▲ The shearer cuts off a slice of coal. As it moves along the longwall face, chocks are put in place above the shearer to hold up the tunnel roof. When the shearer has passed, the roof is allowed to collapse behind it.

◀ A miner checks to make sure that the shearer is working properly and cutting straight. Water is sprayed on the coal face to stop coal dust from flying around in the air.

A Wall of Coal

▶ A miner drills by hand. The roof of the tunnel is supported by strong pit props made of steel.

Between the Tunnels

Longwall miners work according to a careful plan. First, they cut two access tunnels about 100 to 200 yards apart at right angles to the main tunnel. It is one miner's job to make sure that the tunnels are being made in a straight line. Then, the miners cut across the far end of the tunnels to connect them. The wall of coal between the two tunnels is the coal face.

At some mines, the miners make the access tunnels longer and longer as they cut more coal, and the coal face gets further and further away from the main tunnel. At other mines, the miners cut the access tunnels first. Then, they start cutting coal at the far end and work their way back toward the main tunnel. Longwall mining makes it possible to mine about eighty-five percent of the coal.

The Coal Stripper

Miners use a shearing machine to cut the coal. The shearer has a huge drum which is covered with steel picks. The drum spins around all the time, so that the steel picks rip out the coal as the shearer moves along. The driver makes the shearer slice through the coal along the length of the seam, or wall which can be more than 200 yards long. The broken coal falls onto a moving conveyor belt. The conveyor belt takes the coal to the end of the tunnel. There it is put into rail trucks or onto another conveyor belt.

As the shearer moves along, it leaves the rock above it without support. It is the **chockers**' job to have the steel chocks ready to put in place. The chocks hold up the rock as soon as the shearing machine has passed. The chockers also inspect the chocks to make sure they are in the correct places.

The shearing machine makes a lot of dust as it rips into the coal. Dust is dangerous. It can catch fire. Also, if the dust is allowed to float in the air, it could get into the miners' lungs and cause illness. To keep the dust down, fine jets of water are sprayed on to the coal face to make the coal dust fall to the ground as a muddy mixture. Workers called pipefitters make sure that the pipes carrying the water do not become cracked.

Chambers of Coal

Cutting coal by the room and pillar method is quick. However, it is also the most wasteful method since only half of the coal in the seam can be mined. Miners use this method only if the coal seams are very thick and they can afford to leave the coal behind as pillars. Much of the coal in the United States, India, and Australia is mined by this method.

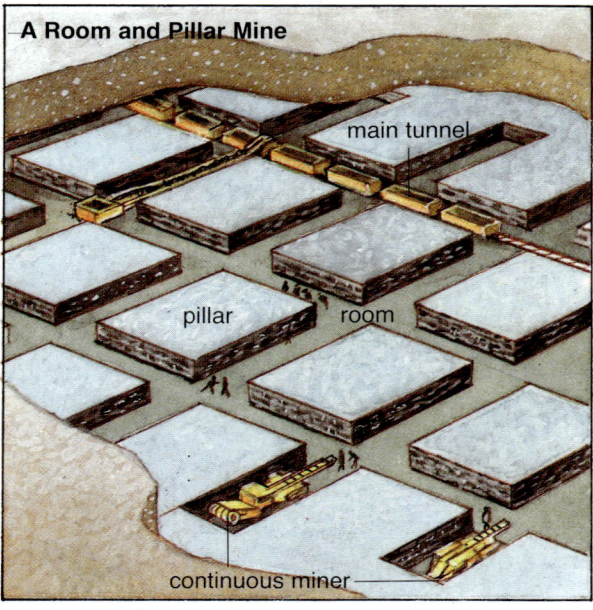

▼ A continuous miner cuts nearly ten tons of coal in a minute. In the past, it used to take a miner ten days to cut that amount of coal with a pick!

▲ A room and pillar mine looks like the center of a new city. The pillars of coal are the buildings and the spaces in between, the rooms, look like streets and roads.

Chambers of Coal

Supporting Pillars

The miners in a room and pillar mine first cut away the coal to make a long tunnel in the middle of the coal seam. Then, they start to take coal from an area at right angles to this tunnel. They leave behind large blocks of coal to hold up the roof. These blocks, or pillars, are oblong in shape and about fifteen yards long and ten yards wide. Sometimes, the miners will dig into the pillars when all the coal has been taken from the "rooms." When the pillars are too thin to hold up the roof, the rooms are allowed to collapse.

Teamwork

Miners use coal cutting machines to strip away the coal in the "rooms." Some drivers can make a machine work by using radio signals. The signals tell the machine what to do. Other machines are more like a tractor with a drill which turns around and around. It is called a **continuous miner** because it never stops. It can tear through coal very fast. As soon as the coal is dug out, huge arms below the machine sweep the coal onto a conveyor belt behind it. A miner in the team shovels coal off the floor, so that none is wasted. Another miner spreads limestone powder to prevent the coal dust from exploding.

Other miners in the team follow the cutting machine. They make sure the roof does not collapse by driving roof bolts into the solid rock. These bolts are between one and two yards long. They hold a steel plate in place. Roof bolting is skilled work. It can also be dangerous. The roof could collapse at any time.

▼ A miner uses a roof bolter. The bolts are used to make the roof secure from collapse.

A New Coal Face

▼ A Polish miner drills holes into the coal face. An explosive charge will be placed in each hole. The wall of coal will be broken up by the explosion.

Miners use other ways of cutting coal besides shearing machines and continous miners. In small mines, they still use picks and shovels. It is not always worth the cost to use large coal cutting machines.

Using Explosives

In some mines, coal is cut by blasting it away from the coal face. This is often the only way that miners can take coal from a seam which is sloped, instead of being level. This kind of seam cannot be cut by ordinary coal cutting machines.

Miners have to be very careful when they are blasting rock. The miners know exactly how much **explosive** to use. First, they drill holes in the coal face. Then, they fill the holes with explosives. They set off the explosives electrically.

Sometimes, the miners use air or liquid gas as explosives. The air or gas is kept in containers. When it is released, it explodes, but it will not set fire to methane gas or coal dust.

As soon as the explosions have loosened the coal, the miners remove it using machines with claw attachments. The claws scoop up the coal from the ground and dump it into waiting trucks or onto a conveyor belt.

A New Coal Face

▼ Miners at the coal face can speak to the control room using underground telephones.

▲ Today, mines have a control room at the pithead. The operator who works there is able to check on work and safety in all parts of the coal mine.

Computer Control

Many coal mines today look more like factories than the coal mines of the past. Some use computers to operate the cutting machines. The machines are run by pushing buttons on a control panel which is at a distance from the machines. This is called **remote control**. The miners are able to move away from an area where an explosion is to take place. When the explosives are set off, or **detonated**, the miners are safely at a distance from the noise and the coal dust. They are also able to work without hearing the deafening noise a coal cutting machine makes when it tears through the coal face.

Underground Travel

Some coal miners leave home every day to work under the sea! They cut the coal which lies under the seabed. The only way they can get there is down a shaft sunk on the coast as close as possible to the sea. At the bottom of the shaft, they ride on an underground train. It takes them to the coal face which can be more than three miles away.

Moving People

Most large coal mines use underground trains to carry their miners to work. The train driver is very highly skilled. There may be slopes and bends underground, and the train driver must be very careful. When shifts change, the train carries miners to and from the coal face. The trains run through tunnels which are lighted by electric lights. Other tunnels which lead to coal seams may not be lighted at all.

At the end of the train journey, the miners often have to travel further on foot to reach the coal face. Everything is pitch black. They see their way with the narrow beam of light from the helmet lamps.

▲ As the miners ride into the tunnel workings, the light cast by their helmet lamps makes patterns in the darkness.

▼ A miner driving a shuttle car with its load of coal away from the coal face.

Underground Travel

► Underground trains are also used in many mines to transport coal and equipment along the main tunnel.

Moving Supplies

At other times, the train may transport all sorts of other things, such as electric cables, timber, or steel plates for roof supports. The train driver must take these supplies to the miners who need them at the right time. These deliveries are planned by mine workers in an underground control room.

Some machines are too big to go down the mine, so they are taken down piece by piece. The train takes the pieces to where the machine is needed. Then, it is the job of mechanics to build the machine.

Keeping the Track Safe

Sometimes the earth moves as a result of explosions or earthquakes, and the train tracks may become bent. If the track is not straight, the train may run off the rails and there will be an accident. People may be hurt. **Track layers** make sure that the trains can run safely on level tracks. When tracks need to be relaid, these workers will make sure that the rails are replaced safely and correctly.

Keeping the Miners Safe

Every time a driver carries people on the train, special safety rules must be followed. First, the driver tests the train's brakes. Then he checks to see if there is enough fuel, if it is a train which uses diesel fuel. Even the warning horn must be tested.

When the train is running, the driver must not drive too fast. When the train carries passengers, there is usually a speed limit of about twelve miles per hour. When the train carries goods, the speed limit is only about five miles per hour.

Coming off Shift

▼ Miners used to return home with their faces and clothes blackened by coal. Now, they can wash up in the pithead showers.

The miners' shift is over! For seven or eight hours, these miners have been working in dusty, dark, and sometimes narrow tunnels. Now, it is time to get into the cage to return to the surface.

At the pithead, the miners hand in their tally counters and their helmet lamps. The lamps must be ready for use on the next shift. Then, the miners remove their dirty clothes and take a hot shower to get rid of the grime and coal dust. They clean their boots on revolving brushes to scrub off the dirt. They leave the coal mine in ordinary clothes.

▼ A mining town often grows up beside the mine. The miners and their families form a close community.

Coming off Shift

A Mining Town

The miners from the same coal mine often live in the same town. The mine may be the reason why the town was started. In North America, mine owners set up camps for their miners, and the towns or communities grew from those camps.

All miners face risks in their work. They depend on other workers for their safety, and for help if there is an accident. Most miners belong to the same **labor union**, which works for better pay and safer mines. When they are not working, miners may join the same clubs in their town. Some of them might play on the same sports team.

Miners' families get to know each other and they also share the same interests. They also face the same risks. Their relatives may become sick from working in the mine. They may lose their jobs if the mine is closed, or even their lives if there is an accident. Families who share the same risks and enjoy the same pastimes form very close communities.

▼ Miners parade through the streets at the Durham Miners' Gala, in England. This annual miners' festival is a labor union rally and a special day for the entire family.

Coal near the Surface

▼ In a drift mine, the miners tunnel directly into the coal seam from the pit head. In a slope mine, they use a sloping shaft to reach the coal seams beneath the surface. The coal need not be lifted up the shaft as it is in a deep pit.

Some miners work in pits where the coal is near the surface. Their job is still hard to do, but it is not as dangerous as mining in a deep pit. Roof cave-ins in these shallow mines are less likely, and the mine will not flood easily. Therefore, the miners are not in as much danger of being trapped in the pit.

The cheapest coal to mine is usually in these shallow coalfields. Miners can put the coal they have cut on conveyor belts which take it directly to the pithead. It does not have to be taken up the mine shaft in skips.

Shallow Mines

When the coal seams are not very deep, mines can be built with sloping, or angled, shafts. They do not have to go straight down into the ground. These mines are called **slope mines**.

Drift mines can also have tunnels which are on the same level as the coal seam. The miners enter the seam where it reaches the surface of the ground.

Miners travel to work on small trains. They do not have to go down a deep shaft in a cage. There is no winding gear in a shallow mine.

Miners cut the coal at the coal face in the same way as in deep mines. They use shearing machines to break up the coal seams. Then, the coal goes straight to the surface. There are no miners whose job it is to load the coal into skips and send the skips up the mine shaft. This cuts down the cost of mining the coal.

Coal near the Surface

▲ At this Scottish drift mine, the mine shaft goes straight into the seam of coal.

▶ In a drift mine, the tunnel may go straight into the side of a hill. The coal can simply be carried out along a conveyor belt.

Old and New Slope Mines

Some of the first coal mines were like these slope or drift mines. The miners often dug into the ground or into a hillside where they saw coal seams disappearing into the side of a hill. Today, one of the longest slope mines is at Longannet in Scotland. The conveyor belt to the pithead is about six miles long. It carries more than two million tons of coal every year.

Coal at the Surface

Miners who take coal from seams which are very near the surface have different jobs from those who work below ground. They are still mining coal, but they are working with machines in the open air. They have to remove only a thin strip of earth and rock before they can dig out the coal. This is called **strip mining** or **opencast mining**.

Stripping the Land

Miners call their work strip mining because they take away the earth in long strips. Some miners operate bulldozers which remove the top layer of earth. This **topsoil** is put in a pile. It is good soil for growing crops, and it will be put back after the coal has been taken out.

When the topsoil has been removed, there may still be a layer of rock and stones on top of the coal seam. The topsoil and rock over the coal are called the **overburden**. Miners loosen this with explosives, then they move it away. They use giant digging machines called **bucket wheel excavators** to take out the earth. These machines have huge buckets attached to a wheel. As the wheel turns, the buckets scoop out the earth. Each bucket may hold several hundred tons of earth.

Another miner may operate a **dragline excavator**. This machine also digs out earth. It drags buckets through the earth until they are full. Then, it lifts them and swings them upside down over the pile of earth.

Cutting the Coal

When the coal has been uncovered, the miners dig it out with excavators. One of the biggest excavators can take out about 2,000 tons of coal a day. Miners either load the coal straight onto the dump trucks or onto a conveyor belt which takes it to the trucks. Then, it goes to the pithead where it will be washed and separated before it is sold.

◀ Lignite, or brown coal, has been excavated in long strips at this opencast mine. This has left behind a series of terraces.

Coal at the Surface

Putting Back the Soil

Strip mining can destroy good land. If the miners left the holes open after the coal had been removed, the land would be useless. It would look ugly and the site would be dangerous. This has happened in North America, Europe, and other parts of the world.

Today, people try to make sure that mining companies replace the land they have destroyed. When the coal has been taken out, miners put back the earth and the topsoil, so that crops or forests can be grown in it again.

Advantages

Surface mining has many advantages for mine workers. There is no danger from roof cave-ins or sudden flooding, and miners do not spend a long time traveling to the coal face, then working in dark, hot tunnels. They can cut much more coal in a shift than they can in a deep mine.

Surface seams of coal are often up to 250 yards thick. Surface coal is cheaper to mine than deep coal. Miners dig out nearly half the coal mined in the U.S. in this way.

▲ This huge bucket-wheel excavator is used to scoop up lignite at a German opencast mine.

▼ An enormous dragline excavator grabs coal and swings it through the air. It releases its load into a truck.

▲ A coal truck is loaded at an Australian opencast mine. Compare the size of its giant wheels with the driver's cab.

Emergency!

The sound of a tolling church bell or a wailing siren was often the way in which the people of a mining town knew of a disaster in one of the local pits.

Anxious families ran to the pithead. Off-duty miners went down the mine to help with the rescue work. Worried onlookers waited for news. Scenes like this are rarer today, although they do still happen. Coal mining is much safer now than it was in the past.

The Safety Plans

Even though coal mining is safer today, it is still a dangerous job. About 200 miners are killed and another 10,000 are injured each year in the United States. About half of these accidents are due to rockfalls.

All miners are trained to know what to do if there is an emergency. Each mine has its own plan and everyone knows what he or she must do. The mine safety committee decides how the emergency plan will work, and makes any changes when there are new tunnels or coal faces. The mines often have safety drills so that the miners can practice getting out of the pit quickly. Their lives may depend on knowing exactly what to do.

◀ A mine rescue worker tests his breathing apparatus before going underground. He is prepared to risk his life in order to save fellow miners.

Emergency!

Miners also know how to give first aid. They may have to do this before the rescue teams can reach them. Some miners have special training, so that they can help the rescue teams. They can use the **breathing apparatus** which is needed when there are poisonous gases in the air. They also learn how to fight fires underground.

Rescue Teams

Many people come to help in an emergency. Doctors, nurses, fire fighters, the Red Cross, ambulance crews, and the police. They work with the miners to rescue the workers who are trapped or hurt. The mine safety officials make sure that they all work together quickly. They **coordinate** the rescue work.

Some people in the rescue team take care of the families and friends who are waiting for news. They try to comfort them, and they make sure that they are taken care of. This is a very important part of any emergency service.

▲ This time it is only a training session. Next time the fire could be a real one. Mine rescue workers must learn to deal with any emergency.

▼ Rescue workers must learn how to treat injured miners and how to bring them to the surface on stretchers. The patient is given air from a breathing apparatus.

Separating and Cleaning Coal

Many mine workers work in the buildings at the pithead. Managers, secretaries, and clerks help the coal mine officials to run the coal mine. Cooks, shower room attendants, and medical aides look after the miners when they come up from the coal face. Janitors and caretakers make sure the mine buildings are clean and neat. Other people who work at the pithead, separate and clean the coal when it reaches the surface.

Getting Rid of Waste

The workers in the coal preparation plant check the coal as it passes along conveyor belts and through the separating and cleaning machines. They control some of this work by computers. This is why many of these workers dress in white overalls instead of in dark protective clothing.

The coal comes to the surface in skips or on conveyor belts. Although it looks like coal, it is really a mixture of coal, lumps of stone and earth, and sometimes even bits of metal. For every three tons of coal, there may be another ton of waste. This waste material must be removed before the coal can be sold. The workers watch as the machines pick out metal bits from the coal. They have huge **magnets** which attract the metal as it passes on the conveyor belt. Workers also supervise the machines as the coal passes through high-speed water sprays. The jets of water wash out dirt and stones. When it is cleaned, the coal is separated into different sizes — dust, boulders, and lumps.

▼ The material which comes to the surface may be a mixture of soil, coal, and useless rocks. It must be sorted.

Separating and Cleaning Coal

▲ Coal is cleaned and graded by machines which are operated by workers at the pithead.

Separating the Coal

Special screens called **riddles**, are used to separate the different sizes of coal and the coal dust into piles. This process is called **grading**.

The mine workers grade the coal by sending it on the conveyor into the giant riddles which shake up the coal. The riddles are made of wire or metal and have holes in them which are all the same size. Only the pieces of coal which are smaller than these holes can fall through the riddle. The coal is riddled several times, so that small coal drops through and leaves bigger lumps behind. When the coal has been graded, it is sold to different customers. A power plant may want crushed coal to burn in order to make electricity. Other customers may want coal of different sizes.

Moving Coal

Thousands of other people have jobs connected with coal, even though they may work hundreds of miles away from the coal field. These are the people who transport the coal, and who buy and sell the coal.

Sending Coal Overland

Coal is heavy and bulky. It is an awkward shape to store and to transport. The sales workers at the mine must find the cheapest way of taking the coal to the people who are buying it. This is why much of the world's coal travels by train. Often, the coal is stored at the mine in a large tower which stands across the railroad track. The coal in this tower is fed into **hopper** cars on special coal trains. The drivers of some of these trains never stop their trains to load the coal. Instead, the coal is loaded into the hopper cars while the train is moving. The driver can take on about 1,000 tons of coal in less than one hour.

At the power plant, the bottoms of the hopper cars open to unload the coal. The train still continues to move forward. Then, the driver returns with an empty train to get another load of coal. Coal can also be transported in big trucks.

▲ This rail track passes close to the pithead. Coal is tipped from the storage tower straight into the hopper trucks.

▼ A bulk carrier is loaded with American coal at Los Angeles. Ships like this can carry thousands of tons at a time.

Moving Coal

▲ Coal may be moved along rivers and canals by barges. Power plants must be sited near to a rail, road, or river link if they are to burn coal.

Coal by Water

Some of the world's coal is carried by water. Dock workers help unload the coal from the trains onto the boats. Coal **barges** go up and down the Rhine River in West Germany. They take coal from France, Germany, and Switzerland to the seaport of Rotterdam in the Netherlands. About a tenth of all the coal produced in the United States is also carried by barge. Countries like Australia have more coal than they need, so they send it by sea to countries without coal, such as Japan. The coal is driven by train or truck to a port and then loaded through hoppers into a large ship called a **bulk carrier**.

Flowing Coal

Some coal is even carried by **pipeline**. For example, the Black Mesa pipeline takes coal from Arizona to southern Nevada. Coal workers in Arizona first crush the coal into powder and then mix it with water to make a material called **slurry**. On its arrival in Nevada, workers whirl the liquid coal around and around in a drum to get rid of the water. The coal powder left over is burned in a power plant to make electricity.

The End of the Journey

The main users of coal are the power plants which make electricity. Power plant workers crush the coal into powder and feed it into boilers which make steam. The steam turns the blades of machines called **turbines** which make the electricity. Coal is also used in iron, steel and gas works, and chemical plants, too. These are industrial uses. Sometimes, coal is also burned to heat people's homes. This is a domestic use.

Restoring the Land

▼ Uneven surfaces and damaged buildings are problems in places where there are old mines. The coal was mined at a time when people did not think, or care, about what might happen above the mine.

Mining changes the use and the look of the land. Strip mining destroys farmland and forests. When the tunnels collapse, in underground mines they can make the rock above them sink or crack. This is called **subsidence**. Subsidence makes hollows in roads and in fields. These hollows often fill up with water. Subsidence is also a danger to houses. It can cause cracks in walls.

Subsidence is most often a problem in coal fields which use the longwall mining method. It is less of a problem in mines which use the room and pillar method because the blocks of coal which are not dug out hold up the rocks. Even in areas where longwall mining is used, the miners leave some areas unmined. On the new Selby coalfield in England, the miners will leave large pillars of coal in the ground below buildings in the town of Selby.

Heaps of Waste

The stones and earth which are washed out of the coal at the pithead are often piled up in heaps near the mines where they form small hills, called **slag heaps**. Today these slag heaps are often planted with grass, trees, and bushes. This makes them safer, as the plant roots help to hold the soil together. It also makes the area look more attractive. However, in some places, this cannot be done because the slag heaps contain many small pieces of coal which can catch fire. In Pennsylvania, some anthracite slag heaps are still on fire many years after they first began to burn.

However, the waste material on the heaps can sometimes be used by construction companies. They use the waste material from the slag heaps to form the foundations for roads.

Restoring the Land

Surface Scars

Strip mining has caused the biggest problems. Strip mines in the past left ugly scars on fields and hillsides. Forests were cut down and the land was left bare with ditches and huge slag heaps in between. Nobody tried to restore or repair the land to make it look good again.

Today, the mining companies in most countries in the world must restore the land after they have taken out the coal. Surveyors help to draw up plans for this work. In some areas, such as West Germany, farmers can grow crops again only two or three years after their land has been mined. In other mines, the water which is used to wash the coal may be cleaned and returned to local rivers. In some places, lakes have been made to take the place of an abandoned mine.

▲ The bulldozers move in. Old slag heaps must be made safe and pleasant to look at.

▼ Once this green field was the site of a slag heap from a mine. Today, the land can again be used for farming.

The Hidden Cost of Coal

Can you imagine the world without coal? Where would all the electricity come from? Many extra power plants which use other fuels, such as nuclear power and water to make electricity, would have to be built to make up for all the electricity which now comes from coal. This would make electricity very expensive. Many factories use a lot of electricity, so the goods they produce would be more expensive to make. This would make them more expensive to buy.

Mining Problems

Coal costs more than money. There are other ways in which coal mining can affect people. Power plants which burn coal make smoke and fumes which poison plants and trees. Thirty years ago, many people died in London after breathing in smoke from coal fires. The smoke turned into poisonous fog.

Miners and their families, and the people who live in mining towns have also paid a heavy price. One of the worst mining disasters happened in South Wales in 1966. The people of the small town of Aberfan suffered a terrible tragedy when a slag heap collapsed. It buried a local school, and killed many of the children and their teachers.

Miners have become sick as a result of working in a pit. Before there were strict safety rules in mines, many workers breathed in coal dust all the time. The diseases caused by coal dust have ruined their ability to breathe properly. Some miners suffer from a disease called **black lung**. Others have **silicosis** which also affects breathing. There are other diseases, such as bronchitis or asthma, which have been made worse by coal dust.

▼ Coal heating was used to heat homes for hundreds of years. Coal fires give out a warm glow, and are still popular in many countries.

The Hidden Cost of Coal

▼ A photograph showing pieces of black coal dust in a miner's lungs. This makes breathing difficult, and may cause disease as miners get older.

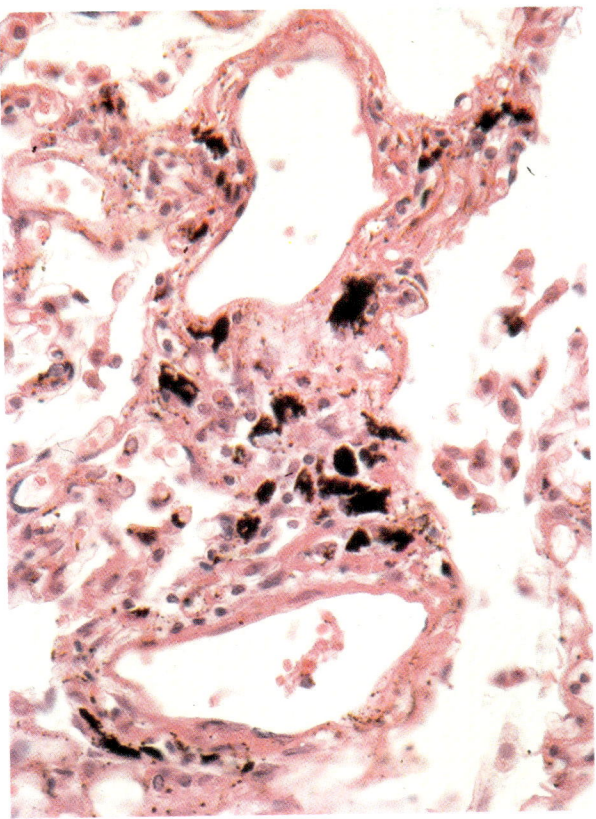

When the Coal Runs Out

Miners cannot be sure that they will always have a job in the same pit. When the coal has all been dug out, the mine has to close.

Mining communities suffer great hardship when a local coal mine closes. The closing of the mine also affects many other people, along with the miners and their families. The miners spend their money in the town's stores. They use the local banks and gas stations. When they lose their jobs, they do not have much money to spend, so the local business people suffer, too. If the stores do not sell much, there will be no need for many store workers. Local businesses may have to close down, along with the mine.

Some people may have to move to other towns to find jobs in other mines, but older miners may not be able to find work at all. When people move away, the town changes. It is not the close community which it once was.

Some miners find new jobs. They stay in their towns and start other businesses. Working together at these new jobs can give the miners and the town a new kind of life.

▶ In many towns, nearly all the workers are miners. When a mine is closed down, there can be a lot of unemployment. The miners have less money to spend, and so stores and other businesses are forced to close down, too.

The Future

Thirty years ago, many people thought that the work of the coal miner was coming to an end. They said that coal mines would not be needed in the future. They thought that **oil** and **natural gas**, which are also fossil fuels, were cheaper and simpler to use and would take the place of coal as the fuels of the future. They were wrong.

Coal is important today, and there is still plenty of coal left to be mined. World supplies of oil and gas are being used at such a rapid rate that there may be little gas or oil for people to use a hundred years from now.

Finding New Coal

This is why the geologists still search for coal. Many people think that the coalfields of the future lie under the seabed. We already know there are large deposits of coal there. The main problem is finding out how to build a coal mine in the middle of the sea.

Other coal mines of the future will also be located in remote places. One day, there may even be coal mines in the Arctic.

▼ A ship searches for coal beneath the sea. A drill is used to take samples from below the seabed. There may be large reserves of coal in rocks below many seas around the world.

The Future

▼ In the future, all kinds of automatic machines and robots may be used to mine coal.

Mining by Remote Control

Computers are already used by mine workers in many coal mines in the United States, Britain, and the U.S.S.R. Many of the machines that are used to cut coal in the mines are semi-automatic. They can steer themselves by using sensors to measure the thickness of the coal seam. Remote controlled shearers are already in use. Systems like this will make the work of miners much easier in the future.

Maybe, someday people will not work at the coal face. **Robots** will mine the coal underground while the miners on the surface control them.

People may invent all kinds of new, safer ways of mining coal. Whatever they do invent, coal mining will be part of the world of work for a long time to come.

▼ The mines of the future will be safer, but will employ fewer workers. The pithead control room may one day be the only part of the mine where people are employed.

Glossary

anthracite: a hard, shiny black coal, containing 94% carbon and 3% oxygen. It is smokeless and burns very slowly.
barge: a flat-bottomed boat. Barges carry goods on rivers and canals.
bell pit: an early type of coal mine which was shaped like a bell. It was usually only about eighteen feet deep.
bituminous coal: a soft black coal containing about 85% carbon. It is used for house coal and for making coal tar and coal gas.
black lung: a disease of the lungs caused by breathing coal dust.
borehole: a deep hole drilled into rocks for test purposes.
breathing apparatus: a set up for carrying and using oxygen, instead of air in places where breathing is difficult, such as in a mine filled with fumes.
bucket wheel excavator: a huge machine which uses buckets attached to the edge of a wheel to dig up earth and rocks.
bulk carrier: a large ship which carries a loose dry cargo, such as coal.
cables: the steel ropes which wind the miners' cages and the coal up and down the mine shaft.
cage: the elevator which takes miners up and down the mine shaft.
chocker: a miner whose job it is to put the blocks of wood, stone, or metal in place to support the tunnel roof in a mine.
coal: a hard black rock which can be burned to provide heat and energy. It is a fossil fuel.
coal face: the surface of the coal seam which is being cut by the miners.
continuous miner: a coal-cutting machine which is used in room and pillar mining.
conveyor belt: a moving belt or shelf. In a coal mine, it is used to move coal from the coal face to the mine shaft.
coordinate: making sure that people who have different jobs work in such a way that they help each other.
core sample: the narrow strip of soil, earth, or rock which is brought up to the surface by a test drill.

detonate: to set off an explosive.
dragline excavator: a machine which works by dragging a scoop or bucket through the earth.
drift mine: a coal mine reached by a long tunnel from the surface, instead of a vertical mine shaft.
drilling rig: a large metal tower which holds a rock drill steady as it bores into the ground.
explosive: gunpowder or any other material which is used to blow up something.
faceworker: a miner who works at the coal face, cutting the coal.
first aid: quick help for someone who is injured or sick.
folded: describes rocks which have been pushed up and bent over.
fossil fuel: material which can be burned that comes from the remains of animals and plants that lived millions of years ago. Coal and oil are fossil fuels.
geologist: a scientist who studies the rocks and history of the earth.
grading: separating coal by putting all the different sized pieces in piles, small, medium, large, and so on.
hopper: a tank or truck which fills up from a funnel above it. It unloads through a flap in the bottom of the truck.
labor union: a group of workers in the same industry who join together to work for better pay and working conditions.
lignite: brown coal. It crumbles easily and looks like wood. It has about 70% less carbon and about 25% more oxygen than black coal.
longwall mining: a method of mining by which coal is taken from a long wall of coal.
magnet: a piece of metal that can attract objects made of iron or steel towards it.
methane gas: a gas found in coal seams. The gas comes from the plants which turned into coal.
natural gas: a mixture of gases, mostly methane. Natural gas has no smell. It is used for heating and cooking.
oil: a fuel formed when tiny sea plants died millions of years ago.
opencast mining: a method of mining coal which lies near the surface. The coal is dug out from above.
overburden: the rock and earth above a coal seam which has to be removed in order to quarry coal which lies near the surface.
pick: a tool with a curved spike on the end that is used to loosen rocks or earth.

Glossary

pipeline: a series of pipes usually made of metal, plastic, or clay which can be used to carry a liquid or gas over long distances.

pithead: the surface buildings at a coal mine.

power plant: a large building where electricity is made.

pump: a machine which sucks in water at one end and pushes it out at the other.

remote control: a method of controlling the actions of a machine from a distance.

riddle: a metal sheet with holes in it which separates rocks into two sizes by allowing certain sized rocks to fall through the holes.

robot: a machine which performs jobs in the same way that people would do them. It is run by a computer.

room and pillar mining: a method of mining in which half the coal in an area the size of a room is not dug out. It is left standing as thick pillars to support the roof.

safety lamp: a type of lamp which can be used safely in mines.

seam: a layer of coal.

seismic survey: a method of finding out about rocks below the surface by setting off a series of controlled explosions. Instruments measure the shock waves from these explosions as they travel through the ground.

sensor: a machine which can tell when there are changes, such as a rise in temperature or the presence of smoke. It sets off an alarm to warn people that there is danger.

shaft: a deep hole in the ground.

shearer: a machine used to cut coal.

shift: a working time of several hours.

shuttle car: a low vehicle used in a mine to carry coal or miners into and out of the mine.

silicosis: a disease of the lungs caused by breathing in coal dust.

skip: a strong open container used for carrying coal in a coal mine.

slag heap: a pile of waste materials washed out of the coal which has been brought to the surface.

slope mine: a mine in which the shaft is a gently sloping tunnel. Coal can be carried out on a conveyor belt.

slurry: a mixture of water and dust, such as powdered coal.

strip mining: a method of mining coal in which large areas of the surface of the land are dug away in strips to reach the coal.

subsidence: the sinking of the ground after the collapse of an underground tunnel.

surveyor: a person whose job it is to collect information and measure land and buildings in order to make maps.

topsoil: the rich soil on the surface of the earth in which plants grow.

track layer: a miner whose job it is to lay and check underground train tracks in a mine.

turbine: a wheel which has many curved blades. It is spun rapidly by the movement of a gas or a liquid. Turbines drive machines which make electricity.

ventilation: a method of making sure that there is fresh air in a room, building, or mine.

winding gear: the machinery which raises and lowers the cage in a mine shaft.

winding house: a tall tower at a coal mine inside which is the winding gear.

Index

accidents 34, 35
 explosions 16, 17
 fire 16, 17
 flooding 7, 16
Africa 8
anthracite 8
Arctic Ocean 8, 44
Arizona 39
Australia 8, 9
 exporting coal 22
 room and pillar mining 22
 surface mining 33

barges 39
bell pit 6
bituminous coal 8
black lung disease 42
Black Mesa pipeline 39
borehole 11
breathing apparatus 35
brown coal 8
bucket wheel excavator 32
bulk carrier 39

cage 13, 15
child miners 7, 15
China 6, 8, 16
chocker 21
chocks 21
clothing 4, 18, 28
coal 4
 cleaning and sorting 36, 37
 dust 21, 23
 fires 6, 16, 17
 formation 4
 preparation plant 36
 searching for 10, 11
coal face 5
community 4, 29, 43
computer 25, 45
continuous miner 23
conveyor belt 12
core sample 11

Davy, Humphrey 7
diseases 42
downcast shaft 16
dragline excavator 32

drift mine 30, 31
drilling rig 11

electricity 4, 42
emergency services 34, 35
Europe 8, 9
 longwall mining 20
 moving coal 39
 surface mining 33
excavator 32
explosions 16, 17
explosives 24, 32

faceworkers 5
first aid 19, 35
flooding 7, 16
folding 10
fossil fuel 4, 44

gases
 explosive 7, 16
 poisonous 35, 47
geologists 10
Germany 39, 41
grading 37

health 18, 19
Hinkeiko disaster 16
hopper car 38

India 8, 9, 22
iron and steel works 8, 39

Japan 39

labor union 29
lamps 18
land restoration 40, 41
lignite 8
limestone powder 23
liquid coal 39
longwall mining 13, 20, 21, 40

magnet 36
maps 11
medical center 19
methane gas 16, 17
mine rescue team 35
mining camp 29

mining disasters
 Aberfan 42
 Hinkeiko 16

natural gas 44
Nevada 39
Newcomen, Thomas 7
North America
 coalfields 9
 longwall mining 20
 mining town 29
 surface mining 33
nursing officer 19

oil 44
opencast mining 32
overburden 32

Pennsylvania 40
pipefitters 21
pipeline 39
pithead 12, 28, 36
poisonous gases 35, 42
power station 4, 8
 moving coal to 38, 39
 power sources 42
pumping water 7, 16

remote control 25
rescue team 35
riddle 37
robot 45
Romans 6
roof bolt 23
roof fall 30
room and pillar mining 20, 22, 23, 40

safety
 clothing 4, 18
 emergency procedure 34, 35
 health and 18, 19
 lamp 7
 mine train 27
 rules 4, 18
 underground 16, 17
seam 6
seismic survey 10
sensor 17
separating coal 36, 37
shaft 12, 14
shallow mine 30
shearer 13, 21, 30
shift 5, 28
shuttle car 12
silicosis 42
skip 12
slag heap 40, 41

slope mine 30, 31
slurry 39
South America 8
steam power 7
steam pump 7
steel 8, 39
strip mining 32, 41
subsidence 40
sump 16
surface mining 32, 33
surveyors 11

topsoil 32
track layers 27
train 38, 39
 underground 12, 26, 27
transportation of coal 38, 39
turbine 39

underground train 12, 26, 27
umemployment 43
United Kingdom 15, 31, 40
United States 15
 fire in spoil tip 40
 moving coal 39
 room and pillar mining 22
 surface mining 33, 34
 upcast shaft 16
USSR 8, 9, 20

ventilation 13, 16

washing coal 36
water transport 39
winding engineer 12, 14
winding gear 12, 14
winding house 14
women 7

48